AERIAL EARTH

Series Editor: STEVE PARKER

DAVID AND HELEN ORME

QED Publishing

Designer and Picture Researcher: Louise Downey
Project Editor: Michael Downey

Copyright © QED Publishing 2010

First published in the UK in 2010 by
QED Publishing
A Quarto Group company
226 City Road
London EC1V 2TT

www.qed-publishing.co.uk

A catalogue record for this book is
available from the British Library.

ISBN 978 1 84835 412 8

Printed in China

Picture Credits

Key: t=top, b=bottom, c=centre,
FC=front cover

Corbis 12-13 Mike Hollingshead/Science
Faction/ 13t epa/ 14-15t George Steinmetz/ 14-
15b epa/ 15t Chris Mattison; Frank Lane Picture
Agency/ 20 Visuals Unlimited/ 24-25
Getty Images 6-7/ 26 STasker/ 27b Sakis
Papadopoulos
Dorling Kindersley 19t
Louise Downey 8t/ 11b
NASA 18t
Photoshot 27 Imagebrokers
Science Photo Library 11 Pekka Parviainen/
13b Gary Hincks/ 17b Lino Pastorelli/ 20t Gary
Hincks/ 26b Gary Hincks
Shutterstock 1/ 2-3/ 30-31/ 32 2009fotofriends/
4-5 Scott Prokop/ 4b Paolo Albertosi/ 5c
WORAKIT/ 7b Tiberiu Stan/ 7t Supertrooper/
8-9 Tyler Olson/ 8b Dark o/ 10 basel101658/
10t majeczka/ 10c Jozsef Szasz-Fabian/ 10b Paul
Aniszewski/ 13c Pavel Cheiko/ 16-17 James
"BO" Insogna/ 18-19 Ramon Berk/ 19 Caitlin
Mirra/ 21 jam4travel/ 22-23 ArchMan/ 23b
Stephen Finn/ 24 Lisa F. Young/ 25b parnick/ 25t
kesipun/ 28-29 T.W. van Urk/ 29 I. Quintanilla

Words in **bold** are
explained in the
Glossary on page 30.

Contents

Climate or weather?

Weather is what happens over hours and days. It can change very quickly. Climate, on the other hand, may not change for thousands of years.

Changing weather

Weather occurs over a short period of time — sometimes, just for a few minutes! In some places, it is easy to predict. In a **tropical** desert, for example, it is likely to be hot and dry, day after day. But in another place, the weather can be much more varied. Most summer days are warm, but any one day may be sunny or cloudy, wet or dry.

This river in Saskatoon, Canada, regularly freezes in winter.

The Sun is shining, but the rainbow tells us that there is rain nearby.

Different climates

The climate is the general type of weather over many years and centuries. In each place, we know what to expect from the climate. Northern Canada has bitterly cold winters with lots of snow. India has heavy rain towards the end of the summer.

Tell me more!

Over millions of years, the Earth has had many Ice Ages. About 20,000 years ago, most of Europe and North America was covered with ice. This Ice Age came to an end around 10,000 years ago.

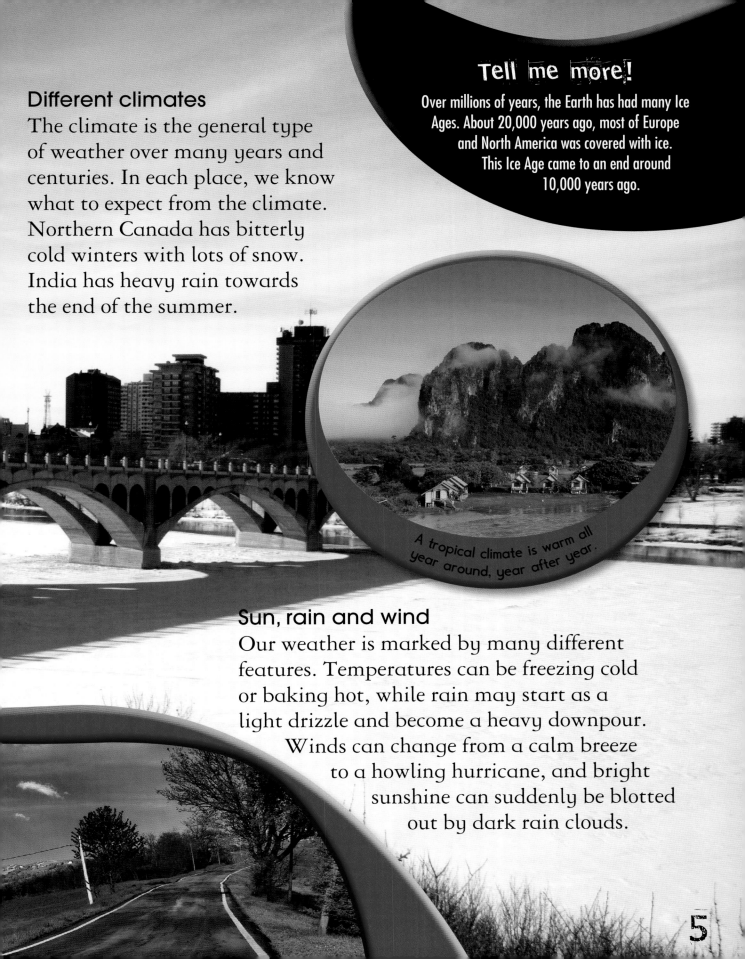

A tropical climate is warm all year around, year after year.

Sun, rain and wind

Our weather is marked by many different features. Temperatures can be freezing cold or baking hot, while rain may start as a light drizzle and become a heavy downpour. Winds can change from a calm breeze to a howling hurricane, and bright sunshine can suddenly be blotted out by dark rain clouds.

Why does weather happen?

The heat of the Sun and the spinning of the world are the most important factors that create weather on Earth.

Our atmosphere

The Earth's **atmosphere** is made up of a layer of gases that surrounds our planet. The atmosphere contains the **oxygen** we need to breathe and protects us from the Sun's dangerous rays. The heat of the Sun and the turning of the Earth make the atmosphere move all the time. It is this movement that gives us our weather.

Wind is the air of the atmosphere moving sideways from one place to another.

Moving air

As the Earth turns, the Sun heats the gases, or air, of the atmosphere by different amounts. As air gets warmer, it rises, and cooler air flows from somewhere else to take its place. This flow or current of air creates winds that vary in strength and direction.

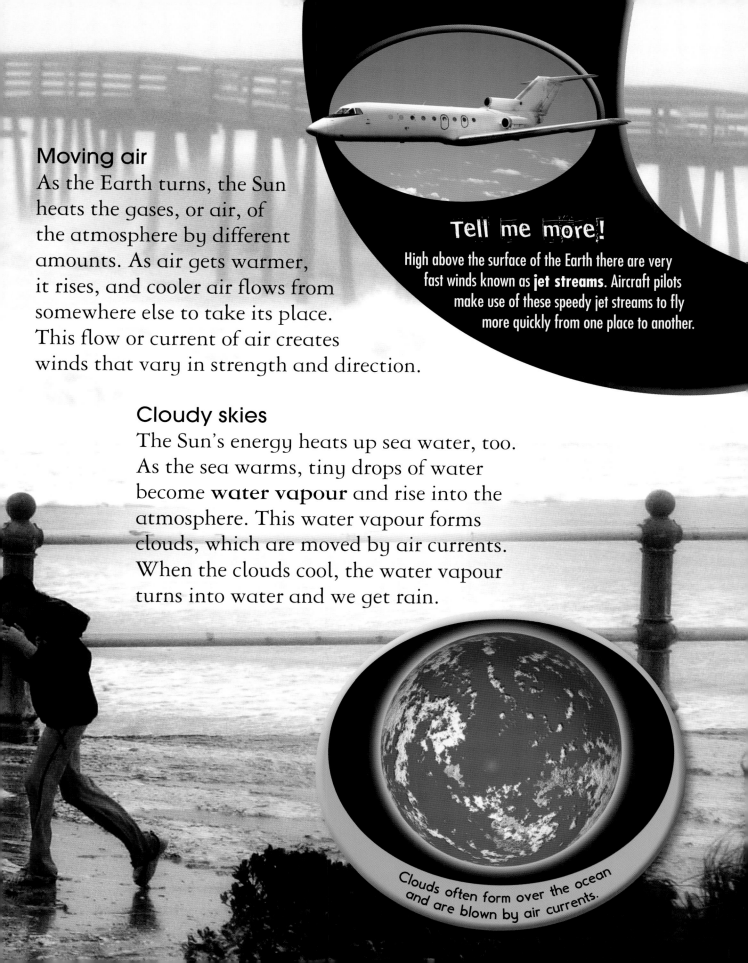

Tell me more!

High above the surface of the Earth there are very fast winds known as **jet streams**. Aircraft pilots make use of these speedy jet streams to fly more quickly from one place to another.

Cloudy skies

The Sun's energy heats up sea water, too. As the sea warms, tiny drops of water become **water vapour** and rise into the atmosphere. This water vapour forms clouds, which are moved by air currents. When the clouds cool, the water vapour turns into water and we get rain.

Clouds often form over the ocean and are blown by air currents.

Hottest and coldest

The farther you go from the middle of the Earth towards its top or bottom, and the higher you are, the colder it becomes.

The Sun's warmth heats the Earth's middle most.

Heat from the Sun

The Equator is an imaginary line around the Earth, midway between the North Pole and the South Pole. On either side of the Equator is the region called the tropics. Here the Sun is high in the sky, so it is hot all year around. Nearer the poles, the Sun is low in the sky and has much less warming power.

Even though Mount Kilimanjaro is in the tropics, its peak is so high that it is often covered with snow.

High altitudes

There is another reason why some places are very cold. This reason is their height above sea level, which is known as altitude. Tibet, which has some of the world's tallest mountains, is a cold country. Africa's famous Mount Kilimanjaro is almost on the Equator, and yet the top is covered in snow!

Land temperatures

Places in the middle of Earth's continents have extreme temperatures. They can be very cold in winter and very hot in summer. This is because the land warms up more quickly than the sea, but also loses its heat more quickly. Sea currents also affect temperatures on land. Western Europe has a mild climate because of a warm water current called the Gulf Stream that flows up from the hot tropics.

Norway is in the far north of Europe and so has much snow and ice in winter.

Seasons

Seasonal changes, which are caused by the Sun, affect many living things on Earth.

Summer

Spring

Autumn

Winter

Four seasons

Between the poles and the tropics are the **temperate lands**. Most of these have four seasons – warm summer, cool autumn, cold winter and warming up again in spring. In tropical places it's warm all year, but there is usually a wet and a dry season.

Spring to life

All living things adapt to temperature changes and the amount of daylight they get. Trees in temperate areas are usually deciduous – they lose their leaves in the winter. Here, also, animals may **hibernate** in winter and seeds will not start to grow until spring.

This photograph was taken several times in one winter's day in the far north. It shows how the Sun rises only a short way above the horizon and soon sets, giving just a few hours of daylight.

Why do we get seasons?

The Earth is tilted as it moves around the Sun once each year. For part of the year, the northern half is closer to the Sun, giving summer here. For the other part of the year, the Earth's southern half is nearer and has its summer. Countries near the poles have just a few hours of winter daylight. On the Equator, day and night are the same all year around.

Summer in the northern hemisphere

Equator

Sun

Equator

Summer in the southern hemisphere

Rain cycle

Water is always moving around and around in a cycle between the surface of the Earth and the sky.

Cloud formation

The Sun's heat warms surface water in oceans, lakes and rivers. This causes water vapour to form through a process known as **evaporation**. As the water vapour rises in the air, it passes through cooler air, which turns the water vapour into millions and millions of drops of water. It is these drops that form clouds.

Heavy clouds gather over the land. In the distance, rain is falling.

Back to the ocean

When water drops in a cloud become too heavy, they fall as rain. If air temperatures are low, these water drops freeze into tiny crystals and turn into snow. After falling, rain finds its way back to the ocean in streams and rivers. In other words, the water goes back to where it came from, ready for the rain cycle to begin all over again.

The village of Mawsynram, in northern India, has nearly 12 metres of rain every year! Nearly all of it falls in the monsoon season, which lasts from June to September.

Ontario in Canada in the grip of winter snow.

Clouds form in the cool air

Rain falls and water flows along streams and rivers back to the ocean

Water evaporates from the ocean

13

Water of life

Lack of rain and over-use of water are turning this Chinese forest into a desert.

Nothing can live without water. But too much water, or too little, can greatly harm people, farm animals, crops and wildlife.

Lack of water

In some parts of the world, such as deserts, it is normal for only a small amount of rain to fall each year. Droughts, however, happen in places where rain does usually fall each year. If the rains don't arrive, then crops may fail and animals may die. When droughts last for several years, all plants die. The soil dries out, turns to dust and blows away.

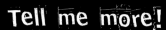

Tell me more!

The spadefoot toad, which lives in the Sonoran Desert in North America, is perfectly adapted to cope with drought. This toad can stay in its burrow without eating or drinking for nine months!

Flooding is a regular problem for people in the Budalangi district of Kenya in Africa.

Too much water

Severe problems can also occur when more than a normal amount of rain falls in a year or over a short period of time. When this happens, the soil cannot soak up the extra water in the usual way. Rivers may burst their banks and flood homes, roads and farmland.

Stormy weather

A storm usually brings dark clouds, strong winds, rain and sometimes thunder and lightning. These are caused by the Sun's heat quickly warming parts of the atmosphere.

Wind and rain

Winds are made up of air that is moving from places where it has a higher pressure to areas of lower pressure. The more difference there is in air pressure, the faster the wind moves. Winds faster than 90 kilometres per hour are called a storm. If warm, damp air meets cold air here, the water vapour turns to rain, which can be very heavy and cause floods.

Hot air rising from this desert has triggered a thunderstorm.

Tell me more!

Lightning flashes move at up to 1000 kilometres per second. They can be as hot as 30,000 degrees Celsius — five times hotter than the surface of the Sun!

Thunder and lightning

When raindrops rub against each other in a cloud they create electricity. This electricity causes giant sparks to jump from one part of the cloud to another, or to shoot down to the ground. This is lightning. Since lightning is extremely hot, it heats up the air around, which expands and forms giant **sound waves**. These waves produce the massive booming sound we call thunder.

This tree in the Lingurian Alps in Italy has been destroyed by lightning.

Hurricanes

The swirling storms known as hurricanes occur every year. When these ferocious winds strike land, they can cause immense amounts of damage and injury.

The strongest **cyclone** to hit Australia in 2006 was called Cyclone Monica.

Terrible damage

A hurricane is a violent tropical storm that forms over warm ocean waters near to the Equator. When a hurricane hits land, it can cause terrible damage. Many people may be injured, or even die.

What causes hurricanes?

Hurricanes form in the summer months. Under the Sun's heat, water vapour rises from the ocean's surface. When the vapour reaches the top of the clouds, it cools and sinks, producing heavy rain. Air currents and the spinning of the Earth then set the storm clouds spinning faster and faster. This forms a typical tropical hurricane.

Winds move outwards

Cold air sinks

Warm air rises

A hurricane forms over the ocean.

A violent hurricane hits land in the tropics.

Tell me more!

New Orleans in the United States was flooded by Hurricane Katrina in 2005. More than 1800 people lost their lives in the tragedy.

Tornadoes

Tornadoes generate some of the fastest winds on the planet. These winds can reach speeds of up to 400 kilometres per hour.

Hot air rising ——

Vortex ——

A tornado rips across the Texas landscape in the United States.

High winds

Tornadoes are formed inside thunderclouds. A column of rising hot air is set spinning by two air currents moving in opposite directions. This spinning column of air is called a vortex. If the vortex reaches the ground, a tornado is formed. Dust and solid objects will then be sucked up by the tornado, causing serious damage. The high winds around the base of the vortex also cause huge destruction.

Spring and summer

Tornadoes are found across the world. Although they can occur at any time of the year, most strike during the spring and early summer. Some of the most severe tornadoes happen in the United States, India and Bangladesh.

Tell me more!

People living in areas where there are severe tornadoes sometimes build a safe room in their house called an in-house shelter. This may be a cupboard or a bathroom. It usually has no windows and a strong door and walls made of steel.

A tornado tore apart these houses in Iowa, which is part of the region called 'Tornado Alley' in the United States.

Five horses

Tornadoes suck up and move heavy objects, including living creatures! In 1990, a tornado in Illinois in the United States picked up a 20-tonne lorry and moved it 350 metres. In Kansas in 1915, five horses were lifted up by a tornado and carried for half a kilometre. The horses were found alive, if not very happy!

Forecasting

Weather experts are known as meteorologists. They have many gadgets to help them predict or forecast the weather around the world.

Highs and lows

Changes in air pressure are very important in forecasting. High pressure usually means calm weather, with warm sunshine in summer and cold, sunny days in winter. Low pressure brings wind, cloud and rain.

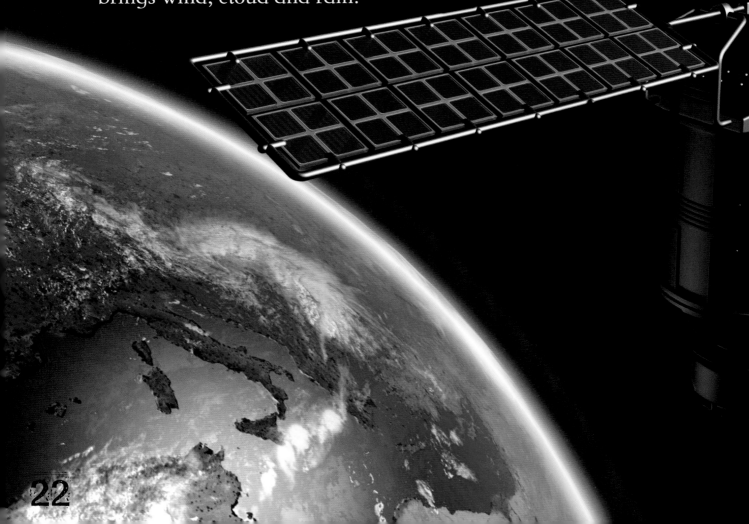

Weather stations

To help them predict the weather, meteorologists collect and process information from weather stations all around the world. This information includes differences in air pressure as well as temperature, rainfall and wind speeds.

Using satellites

Information from satellites has made weather forecasting more accurate. Photographs can show clouds forming and moving. Satellites also measure temperatures on the surface of the Earth and at the tops of clouds.

Weather satellites beam down information about air pressure, temperature, clouds and winds to weather centres on the ground.

Anemometer for wind speed

A typical small weather station.

Wind vane shows wind direction

Solar panel measures the Sun's light and heat

Barometer for air pressure

Hygrometer for humidity (water vapour content)

Thermometer for temperature

Weather warning

People need to know about severe weather,
such as hurricanes, snowstorms and tornadoes,
so they can prepare and stay safe.

Predicting weather

The local weather helps to predict what the
next few hours or days will bring. Wind
direction, the types of clouds and temperature
changes all suggest what is coming. But the
bigger the area, the more complicated it gets.

A meteorologist tracking a hurricane on his computer.

Tracking hurricanes

People who live in a hurricane
area look at the weather
warnings as one of these violent
storms approaches. Forecasters
track the hurricane far out at
sea and try to predict when and
where it might strike land, and
how severe it will be.

Sounding the alarm

Predicting tornadoes is more difficult because they happen without warning. With the help of **radar**, meteorologists can locate tornadoes and **sirens** are used to warn people in danger.

Tell me more!

The Sun looks red in the morning and evening because of its low position in the sky. A red Sun in the morning can mean that rain is on the way. A red Sun in the evening, however, usually indicates that dry weather is coming!

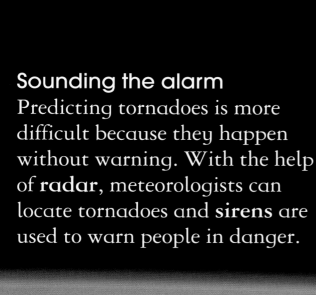

Photographs from space, such as this of hurricane Katrina in 2005, help predict weather.

Harvest time

Farmers rely on dry weather to gather in ripe crops. An urgent weather warning means they can speed up the harvest before storms ruin the crops.

This harvester gets to work before rain comes.

25

Climate change

When we burn fuel in homes, vehicles, factories and power stations, we make greenhouse gases that can cause climate change.

In some areas, climate change may mean that no rain fails, leading to drought.

Constant change

Scientists believe that climate change is not new – the Earth's climate has changed many times. When the dinosaurs walked the Earth, the world was very much warmer than it is today. During the Ice Age, when much of the Earth was covered with ice, it was very much colder!

Greenhouse gases

Today, human activities are releasing large amounts of damaging gases into the atmosphere. These gases, such as carbon dioxide and methane, are known as greenhouse gases. Like a greenhouse, they stop heat escaping. Scientists believe that this is making the Earth warm up faster than it should.

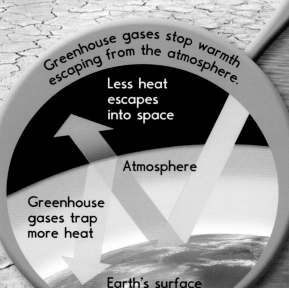

Greenhouse gases stop warmth escaping from the atmosphere.

Less heat escapes into space

Atmosphere

Greenhouse gases trap more heat

Earth's surface

In other areas, climate change may lead to heavy rain and floods.

Tell me more!

Today, around 1500 people live in the Tokelau islands in the South Pacific Ocean. These islands rise no more than two metres above sea level. If global warming causes sea levels to rise, the Tokelau islands could disappear altogether under water.

Floods and droughts

A warming world could have devastating consequences for many people. Firstly, as the world's ice melts, sea levels will rise. This will flood low-lying land with salt water. There may also be more storms and droughts as the climate changes, making it difficult to live in some parts of the world.

The low-lying Maldive Islands in the Indian Ocean are threatened by rising seas.

Green energy

To slow the rate of climate change we must use less energy. We also need to generate energy in ways that do not produce damaging carbon dioxide and other greenhouse gases.

Saving energy

Much of the energy we use in our homes and factories is wasted. We can reduce this waste by using equipment that requires less electricity to work, such as low energy lightbulbs. We can also **insulate** buildings so that much less heat is lost through the walls and ceilings.

Tell me more!

The sea itself can be a source of energy. Engineers are finding ways to turn the power of waves and tides into electricity.

Electricity-generating turbines at sea are sometimes grouped together as a wind farm.

Wind power

Wind can be a problem – but it can be helpful too! **Wind turbines** generate electricity without producing greenhouse gases. Many wind turbines are set up out at sea. It is more expensive to build these offshore, but the wind blows more steadily out at sea.

Solar energy

The Sun's energy, called solar energy, powers our weather and climate. We can turn sunlight into electricity by using devices called photovoltaic cells, which are mounted on solar panels. The Sun's warmth can also be used to heat water for homes and factories.

A solar power station at Sanlucar in Spain.

Glossary

Atmosphere The layer of gases around the Earth.

Cyclone Strong, swirling winds that can develop into a hurricane-like storm.

Evaporation The process of changing a liquid into gas.

Hibernate Sleep through the winter when food is difficult to find.

Insulate Prevent heat or cold from being lost.

Jet stream Strong, steady winds, which are very high in the atmosphere.

Oxygen Gas that animals and plants need to stay alive.

Radar Device that uses radio waves to detect objects.

Siren Device that makes a very loud noise, usually as a warning.

Sound waves Vibrations that carry sound.

Supercomputer Computer that is millions of times faster and more powerful than an ordinary, home computer.

Temperate lands The parts of the Earth that have mild changes in weather between summer and winter.

Tropical Situated on either side of the Equator, around the middle of the Earth.

Water vapour Water in the form of an invisible gas that floats in air.

Wind turbine Tall tower with spinning blades that makes electricity from wind energy.

Index

Ideas for parents and teachers

Here are some practical activities children can do at home or school.

Making a tornado
You will need a plastic jar with a tight lid.
• Pour water into the jar until it is about three-quarters full.
• Put the lid on tightly.
• Swirl the jar round in a circular motion.

Inside you will see a vortex-shaped swirl of water. This shows how a tornado is formed.

Keeping a weather diary
For this project you will need a diary, or a notebook or loose-leaf folder. Children can keep a daily record of the weather in the local area. Alternatively, they could record worldwide extreme weather events and locations, including hurricanes, torrential rain, prolonged freezing weather and so on. The National Oceanic and Atmospheric Administration website is a good source of information about weather events around the world (www.noaa.gov/).

Story of a raindrop
Children write their life story as if they were a raindrop in a cloud. What happens to them when they fall to the Earth in a shower of rain?

Recording the seasons
Children could draw or paint a picture showing their school, house or garden during the different seasons. A longer term alternative would be to take a series of photographs of the same location.

Worst weather
Ask a child to write a story using information in this book about extreme weather events. They could imagine that they have just experienced such an event. They could write this as an internet blog.

Reducing CO_2 emissions
The aim of this activity is to find out how much a child's family is doing to help cut CO_2 (carbon dioxide) in the atmosphere. Using the list below, give a family a score between 1 to 5 for each item. One point is for doing nothing, while 5 points is for doing it all the time. Families with high scores get gold stars!
• Use low-energy light bulbs.
• Re-use glass or plastic containers in the home. Make sure that when you throw them away they are put in the right recycling bins.
• Do not waste food or water.
• Take your own re-usable bags to the supermarket.
• Turn off the lights when there is no one in a room.

Weather words
For this game you will need a large piece of white card. Cut this up into lots of playing-card size pieces.
• Divide the cards into two batches.
• Write as many glossary words or terms connected to the weather as you want on one batch of cards, one on each card. You can use the words defined on page 30 of this book, and then add some more.
• Write the definitions of these words on the cards in the other batch, one definition on each card.
• Deal all the cards between two or three players.
• The aim of this game is to match a word or term with its correct definition. Once this is done, the matched pair is put to one side.

Firstly, players should put aside pairs in the cards they were dealt. Then they take turns to select a card from the player to their right. If they make a pair, this is put to one side. The game continues until all of the cards have been correctly paired.

BETTWS

6-7.(?).